Tawanda Prince

Seasons of Myself
Love, Lessons, Loss, Light and Laughter

A Poetic Journey

Seasons of Myself
Love, Lessons, Loss, Light and Laughter

A Poetic Journey

Tawanda Prince

The Good Life COACH

Rosie Lane PUBLISHING

Tawanda Prince

Printed in the United States of America
 23 22 21 20 19   987654321

Published by Rosie Lane Publishing: ***Rosielanepublishing@gmail.com***
Author's website: ***www.Tawandaprince.com***
Coachtawandaprince@gmail.com

ISBN: 978-0-692-97984-6
Book design: Tawanda Prince
Cover design: Kendall King- ***kkproductions.biz***
Back cover photograph: Amadi Phillips
Editor: Jacinda Smith White aka Hope J. Springs

Seasons of Myself

DEDICATION

To my beloved father **Adolphus G. Brathwaite** who crossed the river to eternal rest in 2018.

I thank God that we shared...
Dr. Rollins
Knock hockey
Parades
Bowling
Race cars
The Bronx Zoo
Palisades
Rollercoasters
Horseback rides
Motorcycle rides
The World Trade Center
The Circle Line
42nd Street
All that jazz
Colleges
Cotillions
The prom
White Castle
Singing with Stenson
The Wiz
Birthdays and holidays
The wedding
Graduations
Child births
Surgeries
Book launches
"The Good Life"

Tawanda Prince

ACKNOWLEDGEMENTS

As always, I thank the Almighty Creator, for blessing me with my gifts and talents. To whom much is given, much is required so I thank God for platforms to use my gifts to bless the world again, and again and again.

I want to thank my mother, Rosalind Brathwaite who has always supported, celebrated and believed in me. Although my dad, Adolphus Brathwaite, has crossed over, I acknowledge that his love continues to be a guiding force in my life.
To my children who have grown into awesome adults embarking on their own amazing journeys may this new "season" be the best one ever for all of us.

To my creative circle, *(you know who you are)* thanks for the encouragement, support, laughter, tears and even creative differences that have made us all more CREATIVE!!!

A special shout out to my Baltimore Acoustic Thursday's family who helped me to grow as an artist and loved me through all of my seasons.

Also, a shout out to my Virginia C.I.P.H.E.R Tuesdays' peeps who welcomed me with opened arms. I wanna rise...I wanna be...ACCOMPLISHED!

Finally, to those who were the inspiration behind these poems, thanks for the gifts of joy, pain and **poetic justice.**

Tawanda Prince

Table of Contents

Seasons of Myself

Seasons of Myself

THE REASON FOR SEASONS
"To everything there is a season and purpose under the sun."
Ecclesiastes 3:1

When I was a young girl, I was given my first journal by Mel Branker, my first writing mentor. The title of the journal was, "Seasons of Myself". As the journal was an upgrade from my little girl days of "Dear Diary..." I was excited. That journal contained my dreams, hopes, secrets and truths that I dare not share with others. It was my private place to express my feelings and create my first pieces of poetry. It launched the vision of someday writing a book of poetry that would be titled, "Seasons of Myself".

Fast forward to 2015, I wrote and published my first poetry book, *Nouns, Verbs and Other Words*. Like most poets, I had many additional poems, private thoughts and positive messages to share which led me to this second poetry book. Staying true to the long ago promise that I made to myself, and Mel Branker, this book is titled, Seasons of Myself.

When I think of seasons, I reflect on God's concept of seasons in the book of Ecclesiastes in the Bible. It is a reminder that there is a time for everything and that the bitter and sweet things in life go hand in hand. Seasons are phases that we go through where we experience love,

8

lessons, losses, light and laughter. I equate these with summer, fall, winter, spring...and Indian summer. The poems in this book include various perspectives of all these seasons and draw a parallel of life transitions and atmospheric changes. Although specific experiences may vary, we can all relate to going through stages, staying way too long in some places and the pains of growth from life's circumstances.

Welcome to my world. Welcome to my truths. Welcome to my seasons.

DISCLAIMER-Not every poem in this book is an exact biographical account of the people, situations and circumstances in my life. However, some creative license has been used to convey the emotions, experiences and lessons learned over a large span of my lifetime or to convey a message. Furthermore, any resemblance of people, places and situations are merely coincidental unless otherwise indicated.

Tawanda Prince

WORD LIQUOR

Just wanna let you know
That words intoxicate me
Nouns, verbs and phrases really fascinate me
Spoken and written down really stimulate me
Do they do the same for you?

Word liquor do you want some
Made for a poet's consumption
Word liquor just sounds so sweet
With a vibe and flow that so unique
Word liquor yes I want that
Sippin' pure facts
Wanna taste that word liquor
You know it's true,
I wanna get drunk off you

Can we just sit down and have a conversation
Just take a sip of some verbal libation
Words that are expressing me
And give me supreme revelation
Do they do the same for you

Write it down so I can sip it slow
Intellectual elixir that makes my rhymes flow
Wanna read and write and say some things
Open up and express my inner feelings
Words I love them wanna let you know
Wanna take my time and sip it slow
Word liquor you know it's true
I wanna get drunk off you
(Inspired by the song Brown Liquor by Marc Evans)

Seasons of Myself

Tawanda Prince

SEASON OF LOVE

The season of love is full of heat, passion, connection and of course love. It is a season where the heart is wide open and caution is thrown to the wind. In this season life is experienced on the highest level and the spirit soars on the wings of love. You are at your best wrapped up on the sands of time, flirting with the rays of the sun, or dancing in the waves. The season of love is truly lovely in all its splendor, and you delight in the pure glow of it; oblivious to the upcoming seasons that are on the horizon.

Tawanda Prince

SUMMER BREEZE

Just to be
You and Me
And summer breeze
Sharing space
Suspending time
Unspoken rhythm
Unspoken rhyme

Just to be
You and me
And summer breeze
Sharing the vibe
No words to describe
The music guides
And possibilities dance

Just to be
You and me
And summer breeze
Exchanging intentions
Through stolen glances
Saying yes
Yet saying nothing

Just to be
You and me
And summer breeze
Imagining kisses that
Taste like fresh peaches
Snow cones and forever
With a cherry on top

Seasons of Myself

Tawanda Prince

Just to be
You and me
And summer breeze
With waterfalls from summer rain
And splashing through
The puddles in our hearts
Sharing laughter

Just to be
You and me
And summer breeze
Just groovin'
And swoonin'
And pleasin'
Just breezin'

Tawanda Prince

COME AWAY WITH ME

Come away with me
To a place where time stands still
Where we explore dreams and discover truth

Come away with me
To a place where we are stripped of pride
And devoid of pretense
Where we can see beyond who we pretend to be

Come away with me
To a place where we are not hindered by
The opinions and expectations of others
Where we can truly be ourselves

Come away with me
To a place where we are free
Free to take off our masks
And undress each other
Revealing our true hearts

Come away with me
To place where I can touch you
Where I can feel you
Where I can know you

Come away with me
To a place where I can look into your eyes
And gaze into your beautiful soul

Come away with me
To a place where you are mine

14

Seasons of Myself

Tawanda Prince

And I am yours
Where we are one

Come away with me
To a place where there are no questions
Only answers
And the answer is what shall be
Between you and me and eternity

Come away with me
To a place where deep goes deeper still
And time stands still
Come away with me

Seasons of Myself

Tawanda Prince

RHYTHM APHRODISIAC

And he smelled of incense, exotic oils
And sweet talk
As he passed by
Melodies and cadence
Melodies and cadence

Musical notes dripped from his soul
His gait swayed to rhythms
Of ancient drums and heavenly beats
His horn spoke to me
And called out to ancestors of sacred love
Melodies and cadence
Melodies and cadence

The richness of his ebony skin
Crowned with cascading locks
The perfect back drop for eyes
Deep with visions of
Crescendos and diminuendos
From tribes and generations
Of rhythm and blues
Melodies and cadence
Melodies and cadence

And as he passed by me
Smelling of incense, exotic oils
And sweet talk
Mr. Music man
Made my soul dance
And his midnight black
My rhythm aphrodisiac

Seasons of Myself

Tawanda Prince

YOU DON'T SAY

It's what you don't say
That draws me to you
It's the passing glances
From across the room
That silently whisper my name
When I read between the lines
I understand the depths
Of your gentle heart
And I realize the void within mine

It is no secret that
Love finds its own way
Even when no words are spoken
It's what you don't say
That affirms that I hold
A very special place in your mind
Where you love me
Without hesitation, without explanation
It's what you don't say
That convinces me to believe
What your eyes try to hide
And if you never say a word
...yeah, me too baby

Seasons of Myself

Tawanda Prince

LOVE NOTES...

I wake up each morning with your melodies
As I arise from my **Deep** state of **Serenity**
Your songs touch my inner places
And I smile from my **First Kiss** of the day
I breathe in your essence
Through the melodic chords
The majors and the minors
A symphony that beckons me to enter in

Your music ignites my soul
Vibes musically intertwined
And I **Exhale** because
There's No One Like You
My **Beautifully Brown** morning glory
A Perfect Work of Art
I would dare to say
I'm **Hopelessly** falling
One note at a time

And singing your **Beautiful** melodies
Has become my **Favorite** thing to do
Like eating **Red Velvet Cake** on warm **Summer Nights**
And I just can't wait for **Another Chance**
To vibe with you
Because **Without You,** my musical world is empty
Because it's **All About You**
And your melodies always leave me **Speechless**

Your **Stories in Color,**
Shine with the reflection of truth, the whole truth and
Nothing but **The Mirrored Truth**

Seasons of Myself

Tawanda Prince

And as always **It's Alright**
Because you are the perfect anecdote
For **A Foolish Heart's Lament**
And my days are empty **Without You**
But with you I'm on a musically, **Peaceful Journey**
That somehow makes me **Stronger**

Though **Not Perfect** but indeed
When I **Circle Back** at the end of the day
Makes me **Wanna Come Home**
To be wrapped in your soul
Embraced by your melodies
Kissed by your notes
Lost in your music

*(Poem inspired by song titles from a **Favorite** artist)*

Seasons of Myself

Tawanda Prince

MAKE PRETEND

Why do we pretend we're not lovers
Just friends
Because to be called lovers
Would involve loving each other
With one mind
One body
One soul
And one purpose

So it is much easier
To pretend we're not lovers
That leaves no room
For heartaches, heartbreaks
And misinterpretations

So we don't look at each other when we...
And we don't kiss each other when we...
And we only touch each other with purpose and direction
Never with affection
You don't say my name when we...
And I hide my flame when we...
Cause that would be too much like loving
And we're not lovers, just friends

Friends afraid to believe
That the feeling is real
Or that the need is real
Pretending not to miss each other
Not to want each other
Passing each other much like strangers

Seasons of Myself

Tawanda Prince

It is much easier to pretend we're not lovers
Because then I would have to admit
That my days are brighter with thoughts of you
And my heart is lighter from moments with you
And if we ever become real lovers
I'm certain that I could even love you
As lovers so often do...

Tawanda Prince

Seasons of Myself

Tawanda Prince

SEASONS OF LESSONS

The season of lessons can be ever so joyful, ever so painful, but oh so necessary. Without lessons, we cannot learn. Without learning we cannot grow. Without growing we cannot live. Fall is full of vibrant colors that make a proclamation of the onset of change. The richness of the season is preparation for transformation. This is the season of "falling..." as things either fall into place or out of place. We fall into a season of discovery. Change is inevitable, but how we deal with it is pivotal. As it is always darkest before the dawn, fall sits at the gateway to winter, the darkest season of all. This fall season is a treasure chest where the pearls of wisdom are stored and life becomes richer because of the lessons learned.

Tawanda Prince

FALLING

When things fall apart
It seems like the end is near
But it opens the path

When the path opens
An unassuming traveler
Searches for open doors

Seekers find their way
The path is bright with colors
Leading the way home

Like sightless birds fly
Heading south for the winter
Looking towards the light

The light leads to truth
The promise of a better way
Things fall into place

Seasons of Myself

Tawanda Prince

THAT THING

It finally happened
We did that thing
That would turn our thing
Into no-*thing*
It was the thing
That you and I
Both wanted more than
Any-*thing*
'Cause that thing
Was a forbidden thing
Which made it a
Sweet thing
Can't be beat thing
Trying to swing thing

Yeah, we did the thing
That was the ultimate thing
And zing went the strings
Of my heart
And that thing
Made my soul sing
And my thing fling
Ready and eager to do that thing
Which was the thing that
Turned our thing into
No-*thing*

More than a passing thing
That is now a thing of the past
Cause that thing
Was a thing

Seasons of Myself

Tawanda Prince

We shouldn't have had
But that thing
What Thing?
Your thing, my thing
His thing, her thing
Was mine for a moment in time
But that thing made me cry
And when I try
To forget that thing
I find that I can't think of
Any-*thing* else

Tawanda Prince

MY HEART

You said you were my friend
So I showed you my heart
My soul, my space, my whole
Though fragile, I let you touch it
For I was sure that you
Would handle with care

At first glance
You peered from the distance
Capturing the best side in the light
That light that first drew you
You moved in closer
My heart so unsuspecting
You cloaked your intent
Wrapped in smiles and promises
Of good vibrations
Sheathed in understanding, compassion
And what looked like love

The pretty wrapping fell away
The ribbon you untied yourself
And at the peak of the unveiling
You dropped my heart
And it broke

Shattered fragments scattered
Of what was once whole and hopeful
Now broken and trembling
Unveiled, unprotected, naked and lonely
And I cried as I picked up the pieces
Of my foolish heart

27

Seasons of Myself

Tawanda Prince

SIDE CHICK

She was your
Chick on the side
Your ride or die
Your slip and slide
Your have a good time

Your never can say goodbye
Your hold you while you cry
The never ask the reason why
Just pretend you were her guy

The never gonna be your bride
The one robbed of dignity and pride
Waiting and watching time fly
Always fabricating an alibi

The give your heart a place to abide
The lickety-split supply
The one who believed the lie
The one who was dying inside

Your beauty queen prize
Make the lickin' stick rise
The accept your compromise
On the road to demise

The make you high
The dare to try
Your sugar and spice
Your everything nice

Seasons of Myself

Tawanda Prince

Your chick on the side
Your ride or die
Your slip and slide
Your have a good time

Tawanda Prince

SECRETS

Secret spaces
Secret dreams
Secret places
So it seems

Secret lover
Secret kiss
Secret passion
Secret bliss

Secret burning
Secret flame
Secret pleasure
Secret pain

Secret longing
Secret need
Secret filling
Secret greed

Secret waiting
Secret fears
Secret screaming
Secret tears

Secret hiding
Secret risk
Secret wanting
Secret wish

Seasons of Myself

Tawanda Prince

Secret places
Secret dreams
Secret spaces
So it seems

Tawanda Prince

NOT O.K.

I said it was ok but it really wasn't
It was not ok that your eyes promised
To take me to the moon
But you left me to search among the stars

It was not ok that you called me
Out of my state of peaceful discontentment
Then left the door halfway open

It was not ok that you pretended
That you were like a kid
Happy with your new toy
Only to toy with my emotions

It was not ok that your lips
Promised chocolate kisses
Only to give me chocolate chips

It was not ok that you woke me
Out of an imperfect sleep
Into a sleepless deep

It was not ok that you twisted the truth
To make it fit your circumstances
That I just couldn't understand

It was not ok that you made me think
Everything was ok

It was not ok that you played childlike games
Of hide-go-seek

Seasons of Myself

Tawanda Prince

And run, catch and miss
A game I couldn't win

It was not ok that you made me believe
Yet, with intentions to deceive
You played look but don't touch
Not too close, not too much

It was not ok for you to send mixed messages
With no intention
To mix it up with me at all

It was not ok that you lured me
With your mysterious smile
Only to remain a mystery

It was not ok that like a black cat
You crossed my path
And double-crossed me

It was not ok that you pretended to play
To an audience of one
But love and loyalty didn't come

It was not ok that what could have been
Love and peace became broken pieces
And the empty spot in my heart is still empty

It was not ok that I was not ok
And you were ok with that
It's just not OK!

Seasons of Myself

Tawanda Prince

Seasons of Myself

Tawanda Prince

SEASON OF LOSS

I t is winter. It is cold. It is dark. It is desolate. It is barren. It is without light. It is lonely. It appears to be the most unlikely place for growth. Yet, in the winter season that which is hidden and buried, is being rooted to germinate in the spring. It is in this season of the absence of light, that seeds are strengthened and transformed. The season of loss, is when things are stripped away and you learn that subtraction equals addition. This season of "nothing" is the pathway to "everything". Like in the photographer's dark room the vision is developed when you are in the dark season of loss. When you emerge the shell of sorrow, pain and loss are shed and you breakthrough stronger, wiser and better than before.

Tawanda Prince

WINTER

It lasts for so long
Many things dry up and die
Cold waits for the warmth

Winter is desolate and barren
Cold that chills down to the bone
Causing things to shrivel and wither
Hope delayed...hope delayed

Waiting for signs of new life
To spring forth
Dry and parched
With roots that lie dormant and wanting
Brittle fibers cling with jagged edges
Course textures define the very essence of life itself

Darkness overtakes short days
And even shorter hope for tomorrow
Light has made the great escape
Winter is crisp and the wind cracks and whips
Stillness slowly seeps through
The crevices and overshadows the dawn

It lasts for so long
Many things dry up and die
Cold waits for the warmth

Seasons of Myself

Tawanda Prince

TRACKS IN THE SNOW

Your love left an imprint on my heart like
Tracks in the snow
Giving dimensions to its purity
And like snow there's no security
Yet cold snow leaves warmth inside of me

Snow is pretty but oh so deceptive
Each ice crystal falls like tear drops
Frozen rain which is liquid pain
That even snow angels can't rescue
White is the absence of color
And the absence of love and warmth
Like a snowstorm at the dawn of spring

Like a snowflake has no true definition
So are the dimensions of my love for you
Yet snowflakes only exist when things grow cold
Like our love is frozen in time
Ice crystals foolishly glisten like diamonds
The tracks in the snow make a cold path
That leads away from my heart

Tawanda Prince

TO BE HONEST

To be honest
Though I no longer cry I can't deny
That I love you
I'm no longer chasing rainbows
With dreams of white lace and white picket fences
I can no longer bear your cross
Or satisfy that monkey on your back
You see the light broke through
And darkness is no longer my dwelling place
Once you see, you can't un-see
Once you know, you can't' un-know
So I must go
To a higher place
Where there is no trace of the stench of
Fermented promises, rotting expectations and you
A place where love and truth really are true
A Place where I can find me

The me, that was lost in the fire of desire for you
The me, that existed before the great fall
And before the great wall of deception
The me, that was thirsty
To taste the wine of delusion
The me, that thought that you would love me
And would not be the fool maker
The me that believed with my heart
Not me eyes that saw the truth

Gray hair says I should know better than to trust a thief
Who knocks on the door in the middle of the night
That it is not alright to borrow or lend a cup of sugar

Seasons of Myself

Tawanda Prince

To an unworthy stranger
And as truth is stranger than fiction
I let this depiction of a saint
Baptize me in the murky waters of feel good

And covered with dirt
I emerged with the hurt and broken pieces
Of what used to be my heart
Scales falling from my eyes
As I realized you couldn't save me
Feeling the sting as I breathlessly cling to forever
Forever changed, my crown and pearls rearranged
But I'm still a queen
And it remains to be seen
The beauty that will rise from these ashes

Ashes to ashes and dust to dust
Sadly I must
Add your name to the ex-files
Forever exiled from my precious
With other fakers and heartbreakers
Who will no longer be partakers of my secret sauce
Now I'm the boss
And what I say goes
So you must
Because I can't trust
A liar and a thief
Who stole my belief
In white lace and white picket fences

So I'm flushing the toilet
And taking out the trash
Letting go of mistakes from the past

Seasons of Myself

Tawanda Prince

And although I no longer cry
I can't deny that I still love you
But goodbye!

Tawanda Prince

ENOUGH

I thought loving you was enough
Enough to make your heart melt into mine
Enough to heal your wounds
Enough to erase the scars of past regrets
Enough to turn you around on the road to nowhere
Enough

I thought loving you was enough
Enough to justify the sacrifice
Enough for you to forsake your mistake
Enough to redirect the direction of your immoral compass
Enough to follow my footsteps to step up
Enough

I thought loving you was enough
Enough to make you choose right over what's left
Enough to satisfy internal and external longings
Enough to make you abandon the darkness
Enough to make you cross the bridge to the light
Enough

I thought loving you was enough
Enough to open up the pathway to your happiness
Enough to stop the emotional rollercoaster
Enough to break the cycle of love-hate-love
Enough to create the cycle of love-love-love more
Enough

I thought loving you was enough
Enough to make you stop running
Enough to give you a solid foundation

41

Seasons of Myself

Tawanda Prince

Enough to give your heart a safe place to dwell
Enough to make your dreams come true
Enough

I thought loving you was enough
Enough to grow beyond your pain
Enough to make you whole again
Enough to make me your queen
Enough to rise above the snakes in the grass
Enough

I thought loving you was enough
Enough to change you
Enough to change me
Enough to change time
Enough to change love
Enough

I thought loving you was enough
But it was too much

Tawanda Prince

HE'S NOT READY

He looks toward the sun
Hoping for the light
He longs for the brightness of the new
His heart longs for understanding
And he understands that
Time is of the essence
And what he needs is my presence

He searches for the key
To the door of my heart
That is already unlocked
And open to the pathway
That would lead him to me
He wants to run
But his direction is unclear

So he travels in circles
Ending where he began
He longs to be a part of me
But that's the part that baffles him
He doesn't mean to push me away
But he can't push pass his fears
So he leaves my heart out on a limb...

Because he's just not ready

Seasons of Myself

Tawanda Prince

WHILE YOU WERE SLEEPING

While you were sleeping
You held my hand just like when I was a little girl
I felt your strength
Although you were half in another world

While you were sleeping
I sang memories with sweet melodies
And I thought of all the things you taught me
And the special way that you loved me

While you were sleeping
I prayed to God on your behalf
And my heart ached as I watched you
Show your incredible strength as a man

While you were sleeping
I thought of past bike rides
Horseback rides and holidays gone by
And I watched you cry

While you were sleeping
I came face to face with that which
You tried so hard to protect me from
The pain of losing you

While you were sleeping
I watched you fight like the valiant warrior
That you have always been
Even in your hour of weakness

While you were sleeping

Seasons of Myself

Tawanda Prince

I longed to hear you speak just one more time
Tell me you love me just one more time
Speak my name just one more time in the silence

While you were sleeping
I wondered if you would wake up
Here or on the other side
And while you were sleeping...I cried

Tawanda Prince

Seasons of Myself

Tawanda Prince

SEASON OF LIGHT

The season of light is like springtime where everything is fresh and new. We emerge from the darkness of "winter" and burst forth with the dawn of new beginnings. New directions bloom along paths sprinkled with hope and promise. Eyes wide open to the glorious possibilities that life offers, while at the same time allowing seeds already planted to germinate. Springing forth, pushing through, growing up, and stepping out...all in the season of light.

Tawanda Prince

THE LIGHT

I feel God moving me towards the light
Great stirring and pulling within
Dawns breaking minute by minute
Bringing morning that relieves the night
Dark shadows fall
As the light brings illumination

God is moving me towards the light
As I catch flickers of purpose
That spring forth
And I embrace understanding
As I see the light of the "son"
Reflecting and radiating in me

God is moving me towards the light
To fight the enemy within
To stop turning my face away
And start living in the fullness
Of whom He created me to be
I am un-blinded by the light

God is moving me towards the light
And the path leads me to
The open gate to God
Who created me in His divine image
Handiwork of the Master's hands
Designed for his perfect plan

God is moving me towards the light
The season of winter just a vapor

Seasons of Myself

Tawanda Prince

As light burst forth
I am shielded from the dark
Drawing me to unknown revelation
I respond to the call of the light

God is moving me towards the light
Breathing space that connects me to God
Where I commune with the creator of light
And all things good
The light, the light, the light encompasses all
The brightness of time never ends

Tawanda Prince

GREATER THAN THE SEA

Just as the river flows
I am directing every good thing to you
Whatever is negative is not for you
And will be forever buried in the sands of time
You will be swept away on the waves of divine purpose
And planted on the shores of destiny

With each sunset my light will rest in you
And each dawn will birth greatness
Like treasures hidden in the depths of the seas
You carry my truths in your soul
Multiplying infinite visions and eternal blessings

The waves will never overtake you
River stones may cause you to stumble, not fall
Currents will never cause you to drown
The "see"-weed will not ensnare you
"See"-hawks will never steal your dreams
But your visions will overflow until the end of time
And carry you to the edge of eternity

Because "I am"; you are
Greater is the "see" that is in you
Than the sea that is in the world

Tawanda Prince

THUNDER KNOCKING
AT MY HEART

That day I stood so unaware
How God would keep me in His care
Thunder came knocking at my heart
It was that day my life fell apart
I stood so still as thunder rolled
I held on tight but lost control
My heart was troubled but still it beat
Then thunder knocked me off my feet
My heart began to tremble and shake
When thunder roared my life was at sake
I had no choice, no turning back
Yes, I was having a heart attack

Fear and darkness covered my way
Help me Lord is all I could say
Thunder rolled and death I saw
As life and death battled a war
Death tried to take me but God said no
This is my servant, she cannot go
I have much work for her to do
The plans I have she must pursue
Thunder rolled three times more
Each time leading me to an open door
To step out on faith, with God to stand
And to follow his anointed plan

When thunder knocked my heart I gave
From death and hell my soul was saved
When thunder knocked I had no choice
But to heed the command of God's voice

51

Seasons of Myself

Tawanda Prince

He told me to go out and tell the world
How he healed the heart of a broken girl

After thunder knocked a rainbow came
My life will never be the same
The clouds went away the sun did shine
Now the promise of new life is mine
Each day is a gift I open to see
What God has in his plan for me
Thunder knocked and I heard the call
To God I give my all and all
There is no doubt, miracles come true
Thunder made my heart brand new

Tawanda Prince

OPEN YOUR EYES

When I awoke this morning
And opened my tired eyes
I thanked God for the sunshine
I thanked God for the night
As I looked outside my window
God's beauty shown everywhere
I knew that God was with me
I knew that God was there

As I knelt down by my bedside
And closed my eyes to pray
I knew that God would guide me
Through another trying day
I could feel his arms around me
So comforting, so strong
I knew nothing could harm me
No one could do me wrong

Yes in my room this morning
God truly touched my heart
I felt that peaceful assurance
That from me he will never depart
God is always with me
And he will abide within you too
If you open your eyes in the morning
And see God the whole day through

Seasons of Myself

Tawanda Prince

FREE

FREE to love...
FREE to live...
FREE to serve...
FREE to give...
FREE to trust...
FREE to have...
FREE to bear fruit...
FREE to choose...
FREE to win...
FREE to lose...
FREE to go...
FREE to stay...
FREE to laugh...
FREE to cry...
FREE to heal...
FREE to release...
FREE to increase...
FREE to climb...
FREE to arise...
FREE to sing...
FREE to dance...
FREE to retreat...
FREE to advance...
FREE to believe...
FREE to receive...
FREE to embrace...
FREE to relate...
FREE to dream...
FREE to be...

Seasons of Myself

Tawanda Prince

ONE LAST DANCE

Last night while I was sleeping, I danced with my father
He held me like the days of yesteryear
Navigating the space between the notes of time
Taking delight in his sheer delight
His creation from the Creator
So comforting and reassuring
He held my hands and let my heart run free
We twirled and spun around
In a sacred moment in forever as time stood still
And his smile eased all my pain away
I knew that he had been with God
I knew that he was doing just fine

Last night God pulled back the curtain on heaven
And gave me a glimpse of eternity
A symphony of angels played sweetly
As I danced one last dance with my father
The brightness of the "son"
Reflected in his smile
And the joy on his face as we danced
Uplifted me, reassured and comforted me
Tears of joy replaced sorrow
And hope replaced grief
Daddy's love forever etched in my heart
Though his touch is now just a memory

Yes on some enchanted evening
While I was sleeping
I danced one last dance with my father
He crossed the eternal shores of light

Seasons of Myself

Tawanda Prince

Just to see about me
And to let me know that he had been with God
He was doing just fine

Tawanda Prince

Seasons of Myself

Tawanda Prince

SEASON OF LAUGHTER

There is a season in life that is neither hot nor cold; wrong nor right; good nor bad...it just is what it is. This is a season of reflection which opens space for you to take an honest look and laugh at yourself or the people, situations and occurrences in our lives. Sometimes we laugh just to keep from crying. Some things that may seem hilarious on the surface are not really funny at all. This season, is like Indian summer; just when you think the season has changed over; the climate reverts to its previous state. Your state of mind influences the lens of your view. Your perspective dictates how you handle circumstances and the climate of the season. Under close examination, the season of laughter brings all of the seasons full circle and prepares you to weather the next season on the horizon.

Tawanda Prince

WEATHER REPORT

Climate changing
Global warming
Hot flashes
Cold shoulder
Artic vortex
Moon rising
Front warming
Clouds forming
Sun setting
Desert storming
Storm warnings
Current raging
Pressure rising
Fire flaming
Spring budding
Sands burning
Leaves falling
Glacier melting
Solstice turning
Water rising
Tide rushing
Jets streaming
Light dawning
Climate changing
Global warming

Seasons of Myself

Tawanda Prince

MR. DISTRACTION

What I thought was a mutual attraction
Was just a pattern of subtraction
Which yielded a negative reaction
So jack you, Mr. Distraction

Of my heart you only wanted a fraction
Which could never bring true satisfaction
Your words never led to real action
So jack you, Mr. Distraction

Your smile seemed to offer benefaction
Empty words were just an abstraction
Merely only a one-sided transaction
So jack you, Mr. Distraction

Pretending you needed real passion
Disappointment was the only extraction
Telling lies was your infraction
So jack you, Mr. Distraction

You wanted benefits without attachment
Desired to play with my contraption
Just a loser's game of entrapment
So jack you, Mr. Distraction

Fabrication leaves a heart in traction
Blocking chances of true love interaction
Fool's gold brings dissatisfaction
So jack you, Mr. Distraction

Seasons of Myself

Tawanda Prince

EXCUSE ME

Excuse me for staring
I can't help it you see
It's been a very long time
Since someone captivated me

And I beg your pardon
For my lack of restraint
But I hold you in my mind
And kiss you once and again

I beg your forgiveness
As I daydream for a while
Imagining we are lovers
As I watch your sexy smile

Would you please be so gracious
As I bask in your glow
And make love to you gently
While I drown in your flow

I don't usually ask this
And I sincerely apologize
But as the object of my affection
Would you let me inside your mind

Excuse me for intruding
But there is no place I'd rather be
Than wrapped in your goodness
While my fantasies run free

Please excuse me for being forward

Seasons of Myself

Tawanda Prince

But some things just have to be
You are just what I've been looking for
Have you been waiting for me

So excuse me is in order
Pardon me just this time
But cold crushing on a brother
Is not considered a crime

It's best to beg your pardon
I promise I won't do it again
It's better to ask for forgiveness
Than to ask for your permission

So, please excuse me

Seasons of Myself

Tawanda Prince

FAMILY REUNION

Come one, come all! It's that time of year
It's a family reunion and everyone's here
We've come from the north, south, west and east
We all get together to meet, drink and feast
Everyone gathers down at the junction
This family put the fun in dysfunction
They say blessed be the family ties that bind
Sometimes family can make you lose your mind

At the head of the table is Papa Joe
He got another family but nobody knows
There's Cousin Jane so proud and uppity
She got her a woman and they live in the city
And Cousin Suzie so holy and true
Had so many men don't know what to do
Oh there's the twins Johnnie and Jack
One drinks liquor and the other does crack
Cousin Ellie, Cousin Dann and little C.C.
Nobody knows who their daddy be
Blessed be the family ties that bind
Sometimes family can make you lose your mind

Big Mama's in the kitchen cooking up greens
Don't nobody like her because she's so mean
Look over there is sweet uncle Clyde
He's here with his wife, but got a man on the side
Oh look over there it's Uncle Chester
Quiet, hush, hush, he's the child molester
Poor uncle Manny drinks like a fish
It's the only way he can live with Big Sis

63

Seasons of Myself

Tawanda Prince

Ronnie, Sylvia and Butch are in town
Gotta make sure we nail everything down
Cousin Mimi is here just as fine as can be
Sorry to say she has a split personality
Blessed be the family ties that bind
Sometimes family can make you lose your mind

And Brother Reverend is always preachin'
But he can't seem to keep his wife from creepin'
Lil' Jay-Jay comes around flashing big money
But everyone knows his paper is funny
And Aunt Louise hasn't spoken for years
She sits in the corner and drowns in her tears
She came with her husband, mean Uncle Nick
He keeps her in check by slinging his fist
Big cousin Lucy only comes just to be seen
Everyone knows she's a fierce drama queen
There's Cousin Ricky who is fond of the dance
It is easy to see there's a flame in his pants
I just couldn't miss this one chance to see
All the nuts and fruits on our family tree
Blessed be the family ties that bind
Sometimes family can make you lose your mind

(See disclaimer)

Seasons of Myself

Tawanda Prince

FLOATING SOMEWHERE

Floating somewhere
Between dreaming and awake
Because this reality I can't take
My dream is dying for goodness sake
Can you help me find a way of escape
The truth is false and promises fake
Just how long does reality take
The journey seems too hard to make
Am I ever gonna get a break
For some this life is a piece of cake
But inside my piece was a poisonous snake

Caught somewhere
Between dreaming and awake
I stare at the walls, is it too late
I don't know just how long I can wait
Breakthrough could take forever and a day
I don't know how, but there must be a way
For ears to hear what my heart has to say
My vision is clear; my purpose is straight
I must change the course of the arrow of fate
So I wait and wait and anticipate
Changing down to up, and bad to great

Floating somewhere
Between dreaming and awake
Breakthrough is just a prayer away
Is there much light in the light of day
Is there any sense in what I say

Seasons of Myself

Tawanda Prince

Do I really have choices to make
Is my breakthrough really at stake
I can't stay here in this dreamy state
Cause most of the time I can't relate
If I must leave then I just might break
So I'll just float between dreaming and awake

Seasons of Myself

Tawanda Prince

CHILD'S PLAY

Sometimes this game of LIFE is like child's play
And I find myself in TROUBLE
It seems to just BOGGLE my mind
That this RING AROUND THE ROSIE
Can leave me playing CHARADES

I often think
Will I just be an OLD MAID
Forever playing RUN CATCH AND KISS
But always falling down the CHUTES AND LADDERS
Never reaching the CANDY LAND

I take my chances using PIXIE STIX
To carefully dissect
The OPERATION of love
And trying to choose the right one
From all the JACKS and BALLS
As I HOP SCOTCH and DODGE BALL
On the MYSTERY DATE, I can't help but to wonder
Will love come NOW AND LATER or
Will I just end up with a MILK DUD instead of a SMARTIE

Will it be another Saturday night
At a table for UNO
Or will I be blessed to
Spend some quality time with a JOLLY RANCHER
Who doesn't think that he has a MONOPOLY
On the MILKY WAY of love
And isn't just some LEMON HEAD trying to steal my
CHOCOLATE KISSES

Seasons of Myself

Tawanda Prince

Which could cause me to
Use a B-B-BAT as a JAW BREAKER
Or even worse,
Use my BAZOOKA to protect my JUICY FRUIT

I believe you should call a SPADE a spade
But sometimes that leads to WAR and
I might just simply lose my MARBLES and
Use some TWIZZLERS to HANGMAN
Who doesn't even have a CLUE

Oh, how I long for the days
When I was a HOT TOMALE
When IKE & MIKE, and all the MR. POTATO HEADs
Were chasing after my MOUSE TRAP
Just hoping to see my TOOTSIE ROLL
All those CRACKER JACKS wanted to
Mix their BLOW POPs with my MARY JANE
But SORRY, I was very selective with my BIT-O-HONEY
And no matter how many love DARTS they threw at me
I would never CONNECT FOUR
Because that only creates a DOMINO effect
And I couldn't handle the SNICKERS from the crowd

However, there was that one time
When MR. GOODBAR's SLINKY
Got caught up in my LAFFY TAFFY
But that situation was just too much of a TWISTER for me
And it caused too much AGGRAVATION
So GUESS WHO jumped overboard the BATTLESHIP of love
Because my heart was torn to pieces in my CHESS

Seasons of Myself

Tawanda Prince

SIMON SAYS that
Good things come to those who wait
So I will have to wait and see
What the MAGIC 8 BALL of love says
Or I could take a chance and SPIN THE BOTTLE
And pray that I don't end up with some
JACK IN THE BOX with ANTS IN THE PANTS
Who just uses my heart for a YO-YO
And leaves me at home playing with my RUBBER DUCKIE

But since there are no guarantees
In this game of LIFE
I can only hope that my PAY DAY will come soon
When I will find my SWEETART
And I won't have to spend the rest of my days
Just playing SOLITAIRE

(The words in all CAPS may refer to a trade name or trademark of certain popular childhood games, toys and candy)

Tawanda Prince

Seasons of Myself

www.ingramcontent.com/pod-product-compliance
Lightning Source LLC
Chambersburg PA
CBHW022130280326
41933CB00007B/618